The

Green Bean

Cookbook

Introduction

Green beans are a tasty and versatile vegetable that are a rich source of many vitamins and nutrients.

Green beans are a good source of fiber, potassium, and folate, and are an excellent source of protein, iron, and zinc. They contain anti-oxidants similar to those found in green tea, also known as catechins, which can improve heart health and help prevent cancer and manage/prevent diabetes.

Green beans are a staple on many buffets and family dinners. They can be sauteed, fried or put in casseroles. They are a great side dish, appetizer or key ingredient in many main course. Green beans are grown in many gardens. They are stored in cans in many pantries and they are easy to find in the frozen food section.

This cookbook contains many of the traditional green bean recipes as well as lots of delicious new variations to try.

Garlic Green Beans

Ingredients:

1 tbsp. butter
3 tbsps. olive oil
1 medium head garlic, peeled and sliced
2 (14.5 oz.) cans green beans, drained
Salt and pepper to taste
1/4 cup grated Parmesan cheese

Directions:

1. In a large skillet over medium heat, melt butter with olive oil; add garlic, and cook until lightly browned, stirring frequently.
2. Stir in green beans, and season with salt and pepper.
3. Cook until beans are tender, about 10 minutes.
4. Remove from heat, and sprinkle with Parmesan cheese.

Spicy Indian (Gujarati) Green Beans

Ingredients:

1 pound fresh green beans, trimmed and cut into pieces
1/4 cup vegetable oil
1 tbsp. black mustard seed
4 cloves garlic, finely chopped
1 dried red chile pepper, crushed
1 tsp. salt
1/2 tsp. white sugar
Ground black pepper to taste

Directions:

1. Bring a large pot of water to a boil.
2. Place the green beans in the pot, and cook briefly, removing after 3 to 4 minutes.
3. Drain, and rinse with cold water.
4. Heat the oil in a skillet over medium heat.
5. Stir in the mustard seed and garlic, and cook until golden brown.
6. Mix in the chile pepper.
7. Place the green beans in the skillet, and season with salt and sugar.
8. Cook and stir 8 minutes, or until tender.
9. Season with pepper to serve.

Lemon Green Beans with Walnuts

Ingredients:

1/2 cup chopped walnuts
1 pound green beans, trimmed and cut into 2 inch pieces
2 1/2 tbsp. unsalted butter, melted
1 lemon, juiced and zested
Salt and pepper to taste

Directions:

1. Preheat oven to 375 degrees F (190 degrees C).
2. Arrange nuts in a single layer on a baking sheet. Toast in the preheated oven until lightly browned, approximately 5 to 10 minutes.
3. Place green beans in a steamer over 1 inch of boiling water, and cover. Steam for 8 to 10 minutes, or until tender, but still bright green.
4. Place cooked beans in a large bowl, and toss with butter, lemon juice, and lemon zest.
5. Season with salt and pepper. Transfer beans to a serving dish, and sprinkle with toasted walnuts. Serve immediately.

Chinese Buffet Green Beans

Ingredients:

1 tbsp. oil, peanut or sesame
2 cloves garlic, thinly sliced
1 pound fresh green beans, trimmed
1 tbsp. white sugar
2 tbsps. oyster sauce
2 tsps. soy sauce

Directions:

1. Heat peanut oil in a wok or large skillet over medium-high heat.
2. Stir in the garlic, and cook until the edges begin to brown, about 20 seconds.
3. Add the green beans; cook and stir until the green beans begin to soften, about 5 minutes.
4. Stir in the sugar, oyster sauce, and soy sauce. Continue cooking and stirring for several minutes until the beans have attained the desired degree of tenderness.

Green Bean Fries

Ingredients:

oil for frying
1 pound fresh green beans, trimmed
1/2 cup water
1 egg
1/2 cup milk
2 cups seasoned bread crumbs
1 tsp. chili powder
1 tsp. garlic powder
1 tsp. onion powder
1 cup all-purpose flour

Directions:

1. Heat the oil in a deep fryer or electric skillet to 375 degrees F (190 degrees C).
2. Combine the green beans and water in a saucepan.
3. Cover and bring to a boil.
4. Cook until the beans are bright green, about 4 minutes.
5. Drain and transfer to a bowl.
6. Cover with cold water and set aside.
7. In one bowl, whisk the egg and milk together.
8. In a separate bowl, mix together the bread crumbs, chili powder, garlic powder, and onion powder.
9. Drain the green beans and toss with flour to coat, shaking off the excess. Dip the beans into the egg mixture and then into the bread crumbs, coating thoroughly.
10. Fry beans in batches so they are not touching.
11. Cook until golden brown and crispy, about 2 minutes.
12. Drain on paper towels.

Greek Green Beans

Ingredients:

3/4 cup olive oil
2 cups chopped onions
1 clove garlic, minced
2 pounds green beans, rinsed and trimmed
3 large tomatoes, diced
2 tsps. sugar
Salt to taste

Directions:

1. Heat the olive oil in a large skillet over medium heat.
2. Cook and stir the onions and garlic in the skillet until tender.
3. Mix the green beans, tomatoes, sugar, and salt into the skillet.
4. Reduce heat to low, and continue cooking 45 minutes, or until beans are soft.

Syrian Green Beans

Ingredients:

1 (16 oz.) package frozen cut green beans
1/4 cup extra virgin olive oil
Salt to taste
1 clove garlic, minced
1/4 cup chopped fresh cilantro

Directions:

1. Place the green beans into a large pot, and drizzle with olive oil.
2. Season with salt to taste, and put the lid on the pot.
3. Cook over medium-high heat, stirring occasionally, until beans are cooked to your desired doneness. Syrians like it cooked until the green beans are turning brownish in color. The idea is not to saute them, but to let them steam in the moisture released by the ice crystals.
4. Add cilantro and garlic to the beans, and continue to cook just until the cilantro has started to wilt. Eat as a main course by scooping up with warm pita bread or serve as a side dish.

Green Bean Almandine

Ingredients:

3 heads garlic, minced
1 tbsp. olive oil
Salt and freshly ground pepper to taste
1 pound fresh green beans, trimmed
1 tsp. butter
1/3 cup sliced almonds
1 tbsp. olive oil
1 pinch cayenne pepper, or more to taste
2 oz. crumbled blue cheese

Directions:

1. Preheat oven to 375 degrees F (190 degrees C). Line a baking dish with aluminum foil.
2. Cut top 1/3 off garlic heads, exposing the cloves.
3. Place garlic in the prepared baking dish cut side up.
4. Pour olive oil over the garlic and season with salt. Fold up foil and seal to create a tight packet.
5. Bake in the preheated oven until a paring knife inserts easily into the center of a garlic clove, about 1 hour; set aside to cool. Once cool, remove each garlic clove from the skin. Reserve remaining olive oil.
6. Increase oven temperature to 400 degrees F (200 degrees C).
7. Bring a large pot of salted water to a boil; add green beans and cook until bright green and nearly tender, 4 to 6 minutes.
8. Drain beans and transfer to a large bowl of ice water to cool completely; drain well and set aside.
9. Melt butter in a large skillet over medium heat.
10. Add almonds; cook and stir until lightly browned, 3 to 4 minutes.
11. Toss green beans, roasted garlic and reserved olive oil, toasted almonds, and 1 tbsp. olive oil together in a large bowl; season with cayenne pepper, salt, and black pepper. Transfer to a shallow baking dish and top with blue cheese.7
12. Bake until cheese is melted and beans are fully tender, about 15 minutes.

Green Bean Casserole

Ingredients:

2 (10.75 oz.) cans condensed cream of mushroom soup
1 cup milk
2 tsps. soy sauce
1/4 tsp. ground black pepper
8 cups cooked cut green beans
2 2/3 cups French's® French Fried Onions

Directions:

1. Stir soup, milk, soy sauce, pepper, beans and 1 1/3 cups onions in 3-qt. casserole.
2. Bake at 350 degrees F. for 25 min. or until hot.
3. Stir.
4. Top with remaining onions.
5. Bake for 5 min. more.

Sweet and Spicy Green Beans

Ingredients:

3/4 pound fresh green beans, trimmed
2 tbsps. soy sauce
1 clove garlic, minced
1 tsp. garlic chili sauce
1 tsp. honey
2 tsps. canola oil

Directions:

1. Arrange a steamer basket in a pot over boiling water, and steam the green beans 3 to 4 minutes.
2. In a bowl, mix the soy sauce, garlic, garlic chili sauce, and honey.
3. Heat the canola oil in a skillet over medium heat.
4. Add the green beans, and fry for 3 to 5 minutes.
5. Pour in the soy sauce mixture. Continue cooking and stirring 2 minutes, or until the liquid is nearly evaporated. Serve immediately.

Arkansas Green Beans

Ingredients:

5 (15 oz.) cans green beans, drained
7 slices bacon2/3 cup brown sugar
1/4 cup butter, melted
7 tsps. soy sauce
1 1/2 tsps. garlic powder

Directions:

1. Preheat an oven to 350 degrees F (175 degrees C).
2. Place the drained green beans in a 9x13 inch baking pan.
3. Cook bacon in a microwave on microwave-safe plate for 2 minutes until slightly cooked. Lay the bacon on top of the green beans.
4. Combine the brown sugar, melted butter, soy sauce, and garlic powder in a small bowl.
5. Pour the butter mixture over the green beans and bacon.
6. Bake uncovered in the preheated oven for 40 minutes.

Lemon-Parsley Green Beans

Ingredients:

1 pinch white sugar
1 pound fresh green beans, trimmed
2 tbsps. butter
2 tsps. olive oil
3 cloves garlic, minced
1 tbsp. lemon zest
1/4 cup chopped fresh parsley
Salt and pepper to taste
1 lemon, cut into wedges

Directions:

1. Bring a large pot of salted water to a boil over high heat: add sugar, and beans.
2. Cook until beans are bright green and tender, 3 to 5 minutes.
3. Drain, and place in a large bowl of ice water to stop cooking.
4. Combine the butter and olive oil in a large skillet over medium-high heat; cook until butter melts.
5. Stir in the garlic; cook until pale beige and fragrant.
6. Stir in the beans; cook until wilted, and garlic is dark brown, about 4 minutes.
7. Toss beans with parsley and lemon zest, and cook 1 to 2 minutes more.
8. Season to taste with salt and pepper. Transfer beans to a serving dish, and garnish with lemon wedges.

Green Beans with Caramelized Onions

Ingredients:

1 tbsp. olive oil
1 tbsp. white sugar
1 (16 oz.) package frozen pear
1 onion
1 (16 oz.) package frozen cut green beans, thawed
1 tbsp. fresh dill weed
1/2 tsp. salt
1/4 tsp. ground black pepper

Directions:

1. Heat the oil and sugar in a large skillet over medium-high heat.
2. Add the onions; cook and stir until tender and golden brown, about 10 minutes.
3. Mix the green beans with the onions, and cook for about 3 minutes.
4. Remove from heat and season with dill, salt and pepper.

Japanese-Style Sesame Green Beans

Ingredients:

1 tbsp. canola oil
1 1/2 tsps. sesame oil
1 pound fresh green beans, washed
1 tbsp. soy sauce
1 tbsp. toasted sesame seeds

Directions:

1. Warm a large skillet or wok over medium heat. When the skillet is hot, pour in canola and sesame oils, then place whole green beans into the skillet.
2. Stir the beans to coat with oil.
3. Cook until the beans are bright green and slightly browned in spots, about 10 minutes.
4. Remove from heat, and stir in soy sauce; cover, and let sit about 5 minutes. Transfer to a serving platter, and sprinkle with toasted sesame seeds.

Pickled Green Beans

Ingredients:

2 pounds fresh green beans, rinsed and trimmed
4 cloves garlic, peeled
8 sprigs fresh dill weed
4 tsps. salt
2 1/2 cups white vinegar
2 1/2 cups water

Directions:

1. Cut green beans to fit inside pint canning jars.
2. Place green beans in a steamer over 1 inch of boiling water, and cover.
3. Cook until tender but still firm, for 3 minutes. Plunge beans into ice water.
4. Drain well.
5. Pack the beans into four hot, sterilized pint jars.
6. Place 1 clove garlic and 2 sprigs dill weed in each jar, against the glass.
7. Add 1 tsp. of salt to each jar.
8. In a large saucepan over high heat, bring vinegar and water to a boil.
9. Pour over beans.
10. Fit the jars with lids and rings and process for 10 minutes in a boiling water bath.

Green Beans with Bread Crumbs

Ingredients:

1 pound fresh green beans, washed and trimmed
1/2 cup water
1/4 cup Italian seasoned bread crumbs
1/4 cup olive oil
Salt and pepper to taste
1/4 tsp. garlic powder
1/4 tsp. dried oregano
1/4 tsp. dried basil
1/4 cup grated Parmesan cheese

Directions:

1. Combine green beans and 1/2 cup water in a medium pot.
2. Cover, and bring to boil.
3. Reduce heat to medium, and let beans cook for 10 minutes, or until tender.
4. Drain well.
5. Place beans in a medium serving bowl, and mix in bread crumbs, olive oil, salt, pepper, garlic powder, oregano and basil.
6. Toss mixture until the beans are coated.
7. Sprinkle with Parmesan cheese, and serve.

Green Beans with Cherry Tomatoes

Ingredients:

1 1/2 pounds green beans, trimmed and cut into pieces
1 1/2 cups water
1/4 cup butter
1 tbsp. sugar
3/4 tsp. garlic salt
1/4 tsp. pepper
1 1/2 tsps. chopped fresh basil
2 cups cherry tomato halves

Directions:

1. Place beans and water in a large saucepan.
2. Cover, and bring to a boil. Set heat to low, and simmer until tender, about 10 minutes.
3. Drain off water, and set aside.
4. Melt butter in a skillet over medium heat.
5. Stir in sugar, garlic salt, pepper and basil.
6. Add tomatoes, and cook stirring gently just until soft.
7. Pour the tomato mixture over the green beans, and toss gently to blend.

Sesame Tempura Green Beans

Ingredients:

2 quarts oil for deep frying
1 cup all-purpose flour
1/4 cup sesame seeds
1 (12 fluid oz.) can or bottle beer
3/4 pound fresh green beans, rinsed and trimmed
Salt to taste
3 tbsps. soy sauce
3 tsps. lime juice
1 tsp. white sugar

Directions:

1. Heat oil in deep-fryer to 375 degrees F (190 degrees C).
2. In a medium bowl, mix the flour, sesame seeds and beer until smooth.
3. Roll the beans in the flour mixture to coat.
4. Deep fry the coated beans in small batches until golden brown, about 1 1/2 minutes per batch.
5. Drain on paper towels. Salt to taste.
6. In a small bowl, whisk together the soy sauce, lime juice and sugar to use as a dipping sauce.

Three Bean Salad

Ingredients:

1 (15 oz.) can green beans
1 pound wax beans
1 (15 oz.) can kidney beans, drained and rinsed
1 onion, sliced into thin rings
3/4 cup white sugar
2/3 cup distilled white vinegar
1/3 cup vegetable oil
1/2 tsp. salt
1/2 tsp. ground black pepper
1/2 tsp. celery seed

Directions:

1. Mix together green beans, wax beans, kidney beans, onion, sugar, vinegar, vegetable oil, salt, pepper, and celery seed. Let set in refrigerator for at least 12 hours.

Creamy Corn and Green Bean Casserole

Ingredients:

1 (16 oz.) can green beans, drained
1 (14 oz.) can whole kernel corn, drained
2 (10.75 oz.) cans cream of celery soup, undiluted
1 onion, chopped
2 cups coarsely crushed buttery round crackers
1 pinch garlic powder, or to taste
2 tbsps. margarine, melted

Directions:

1. Preheat the oven to 325 degrees F (165 degrees C).
2. Combine the green beans and corn in the bottom of a 9-inch square baking dish.
3. Pour soup over the vegetables and top with chopped onion.
4. In a small bowl, stir together the crackers, garlic powder, and margarine until cracker crumbs are coated.
5. Spread over the top of the casserole.
6. Bake for 1 hour in the preheated oven, or until the sauce is thick and the top is browned.

Cheesy Green Bean Casserole

Ingredients:

1 egg
1 tsp. white sugar
1/2 cup all-purpose flour
Ground black pepper to taste
1 1/4 cups vegetable oil for deep-frying
1 small onion, sliced and separated into rings
2 (14.5 oz.) cans French cut green beans, drained
1 (10.75 oz.) can condensed cream of mushroom soup, undiluted
1/4 cup milk
1/2 cup shredded sharp Cheddar cheese
1 pinch paprika, for garnish (optional)
Ground black pepper to taste

Directions:

1. Whisk the egg with a fork in a small bowl.
2. In a separate bowl, stir together the flour and pepper. Heat the oil in a heavy skillet or deep fryer to 375 degrees F (190 degrees C). Dip each onion ring into the egg and then coat with flour.
3. Add them to the hot oil a few at a time. Fry until golden brown, turning once if needed, it should take about 3 minutes. Set them onto a paper towel-lined plate to drain and cool. Chop into 1/2 inch pieces.
4. Preheat the oven to 350 degrees F (175 degrees C).
5. In a medium bowl, stir together the green beans, cream of mushroom soup, and milk.
6. Stir in about half of the onions. Transfer to a casserole dish.
7. Bake in the preheated oven until heated through and bubbly, about 25 minutes.
8. Remove from the oven and sprinkle the cheese and remaining onions on top.
9. Bake until browned on the top, about 10 more minutes.
10. Remove from the oven and garnish with a sprinkle of paprika and black pepper.

Bacon and Almond Green Bean Casserole

Ingredients:

6 slices thick-cut bacon
1 1/2 cups whole milk
2 (10.75 oz.) cans condensed cream of mushroom soup
1/2 cup sliced almonds
3/4 tsp. garlic-pepper seasoning
3/4 (6 oz.) can French fried onions
4 (14.5 oz.) cans green beans, drained
1/4 (6 oz.) can French-fried onions

Directions:

1. Preheat oven to 350 degrees F (175 degrees C).
2. Place bacon in a large skillet and cook over medium-high heat, turning occasionally, until evenly browned, about 10 minutes.
3. Drain on paper towels; break into 1-inch pieces.
4. Stir milk and cream of mushroom soup together in a large bowl.
5. Add almonds, garlic pepper, and 3/4 can French-fried onion; stir to combine. Fold green beans carefully into mixture.
6. Pour into a 9x9-inch ceramic or glass baking dish.
7. Bake in the preheated oven until cooked through and bubbling, about 20 minutes. Top with remaining 1/4 can French-fried onions; bake until onions are lightly browned, 3 to 4 minutes.

Southern Green Beans

Ingredients:

6 slices bacon, chopped
3 tbsps. butter
1 red onion, chopped
2 pounds fresh green beans, trimmed and snapped
8 small new potatoes, diced
1 large clove garlic, minced
1/4 cup chicken broth
1 1/2 tsps. white balsamic vinegar
Salt and pepper to taste

Directions:

1. Place the chopped bacon in a skillet, and cook over medium heat, stirring occasionally, until evenly browned, 8 to 10 minutes.
2. Drain the bacon pieces on a paper towel-lined plate.
3. Melt the butter in a skillet with a lid over medium-low heat, and cook and stir the onion until translucent, about 5 minutes.
4. Stir in the cooked bacon, green beans, potatoes, garlic, and chicken broth.
5. Bring to a boil, cover, and simmer over low heat until the green beans are tender, about 10 minutes.
6. Sprinkle with vinegar, salt, and pepper, and serve.

Green Bean and Mushroom Medley

Ingredients:

1/2 pound fresh green beans, cut
2 carrots, cut into thick strips
1/4 cup butter
1 onion, sliced
1/2 pound fresh mushrooms, sliced
1 tsp. salt
1/2 tsp. seasoned salt
1/4 tsp. garlic salt
1/4 tsp. white pepper

Directions:

1. Place green beans and carrots in 1 inch of boiling water.
2. Cover, and cook until tender but still firm.
3. Drain.
4. Melt butter in a large skillet over medium heat. Saute onions and mushrooms until almost tender.
5. Reduce heat, cover, and simmer 3 minutes.
6. Stir in green beans, carrots, salt, seasoned salt, garlic salt, and white pepper.
7. Cover, and cook for 5 minutes over medium heat.

Sweet and Sour Green Beans

Ingredients:

2 (15 oz.) cans green beans, drained, juices reserved
3 slices bacon, chopped
1 cup chopped onion
1 tbsp. all-purpose flour
1/4 cup apple cider vinegar
2 tbsps. sugar
1 tsp. salt
1/4 tsp. pepper

Directions:

1. Cook bacon in a medium skillet over medium-high heat, stirring occasionally, until well-browned.
2. Add onion and cook until translucent.
3. Stir in flour and cook 2 minutes more.
4. Pour vinegar and 3/4 cup of the reserved green bean liquid into the pan.
5. Add sugar, salt, and pepper, and stir to combine.
6. Bring to a boil, reduce to a simmer, and stir in the green beans. Continue cooking at a low simmer until beans are hot.

Green Beans With a Twist

Ingredients:

2 eggs
2 (14.5 oz.) cans green beans, drained
1 cup mayonnaise
1 tbsp. lemon juice
1 tsp. Worcestershire sauce
1 tbsp. prepared horseradish
1 dash black pepper
1 dash garlic powder
1 dash onion powder
1 1/2 tsps. dried parsley

Directions:

1. Place egg in a saucepan and cover with cold water.
2. Bring water to a boil and immediately remove from heat.
3. Cover and let eggs stand in hot water for 10 to 12 minutes.
4. Remove from hot water, cool, peel and chop.
5. In a large bowl combine eggs, green beans, mayonnaise, lemon juice, Worcestershire sauce, horseradish, pepper, garlic powder, onion powder and parsley.

Green Beans Italiano

Ingredients:

2 pounds green beans, trimmed
1/2 cup olive oil
2 tsps. minced fresh garlic
2 tsps. white sugar
1 1/2 tsps. salt
1 1/2 cups beef broth
1 (14.5 oz.) can Italian diced tomatoes, drained
2 tbsps. parsley flakes

Directions:

1. Stir green beans, olive oil, garlic, sugar, and salt in a large skillet.
2. Place a cover on the skillet and cook over low heat until green beans are slightly tender, about 15 minutes.
3. Pour beef broth over the green bean mixture; continue cooking uncovered about 5 minutes more.
4. Increase heat to medium-high.
5. Stir tomatoes and parsley through the green bean mixture; continue cooking until beans are cooked through and tender, about 5 minutes more.

Grilled Fresh Green Beans

Ingredients:

1 pound fresh green beans
1 small onion, sliced
2 slices bacon, cut into quarters
1 tbsp. olive oil, or as needed
1 pinch salt-free seasoning blend (such as Mrs. Dash)
1 portobello mushroom, sliced

Directions:

1. Preheat an outdoor grill for medium-high heat and lightly oil the grate.
2. Combine green beans, onion, and bacon in a bowl. Drizzle olive oil over green beans mixture and season with seasoning blend; stir to coat. Transfer green beans mixture to a grilling basket or wok.
3. Place green beans mixture on the preheated grill and cook, stirring every 10 minutes, until tender, about 30 minutes.
4. Add mushroom to green beans mixture and cook until tender, about 10 minutes more.

Green Beans with Garlic Dill Hollandaise Sauce

Ingredients:

5 slices bacon
1/4 cup chicken stock
1/4 cup heavy whipping cream
1 1/2 tsps. fresh lemon juice
3 cloves garlic, minced
1 tsp. dried dill weed
6 egg yolks
1/4 tsp. fresh ground black pepper
2 cups chicken broth
2 pounds fresh whole green beans, trimmed
1/2 tsp. fresh ground black pepper

Directions:

1. Place turkey bacon in a skillet over medium to medium-high heat.
2. Cook to desired crispness, turning occasionally, about 6 minutes.
3. Remove from heat; let cool slightly. Chop bacon into small pieces.
4. Mix Chicken Stock, cream, lemon juice, minced garlic, and dill in a microwaveable bowl. Microwave on HIGH for 1 minute, 30 seconds.
5. Place water in the bottom of a double boiler; water should not touch the bottom of the top pan.
6. Bring water to a boil.
7. Lightly beat egg yolks in the top of the double boiler.
8. Cook, stirring until thickened and egg yolks are about double in volume, 3 to 5 minutes.
9. Reduce heat to low.
10. Gradually whisk in stock/cream mixture, whisking until completely combined.
11. Mix thoroughly for another minute.
12. Season with 1/4 tsp. black pepper.
13. Remove from heat and cover to keep sauce warm.
14. Set a steamer basket insert into a large saucepan.
15. Pour in Chicken Broth to just below the bottom of the steamer; bring to a boil.
16. Add green beans, season with 1/2 tsp. black pepper and steam until crisp-tender, about 5 minutes. Discard leftover chicken broth or reserve for another use.
17. Transfer beans to a serving dish; sprinkle with bacon crumbles. Top with hollandaise sauce and serve.

Green Beans and Pears with Bacon

Ingredients:

1/2 pound thick sliced bacon, cut into 1 inch pieces
1 pound fresh green beans, trimmed and cut into 1 1/2-inch pieces
3 Bosc pears, cored and cut into quarters
1 quart water
Salt and pepper to taste

Directions:

1. Cook the bacon in a large, deep skillet over medium-high heat, stirring occasionally, until partially cooked but not brown, 5 to 6 minutes; drain on paper towels.
2. Combine the drained bacon, green beans, and pears in a large saucepan; pour enough water over the mixture to cover.
3. Bring to a boil; reduce the heat to low and simmer until cooked and tender, about 30 minutes.
4. Remove from the pan to a serving dish with a slotted spoon, draining excess water.
5. Season with salt and pepper to serve.

Green Beans with Cheese and Bacon

Ingredients:

3 cups trimmed green beans, snapped in half
3 slices bacon, diced
6 green onions, chopped
1/2 cup shredded sharp Cheddar cheese
1/4 cup sour cream
1/4 cup mayonnaise
1 pinch salt and pepper to taste

Directions:

1. Preheat oven to 325 degrees F (165 degrees C).
2. Lightly grease a 2 1/2-quart baking dish with a lid.
3. Place the green beans in a large pan with water to cover; bring to a boil and cook only until the beans are hot and bright green, about 1 minute.
4. Drain. Transfer to a large bowl.
5. Cook the bacon in a large, deep skillet over medium-high heat, stirring occasionally, until evenly browned and crisp, about 10 minutes.
6. Pour off all but 1 tbsp. of the drippings. Return to the heat and add the green onions; cook until the onions have softened, about 2 minutes.
7. Add the bacon mixture, Cheddar cheese, sour cream, mayonnaise, salt, and pepper to the green beans; stir.
8. Spread the mixture into the prepared baking dish; cover with the lid.
9. Bake in the preheated oven until the casserole is bubbling and the beans are tender, about 20 minutes.

Green Beans with Blue Cheese

Ingredients:

1 pound fresh green beans, cut into 2 inch pieces
1/4 cup bacon drippings
3 oz. crumbled blue cheese
1/2 cup chopped walnuts, toasted
Salt and pepper to taste

Directions:

1. Place green beans in a saucepan with one inch of water in the bottom.
2. Bring to a boil over medium-high heat, and cook for 5 minutes, or until tender-crisp.
3. Remove from heat, drain, and set aside.
4. Heat the bacon drippings in a large skillet over medium heat.
5. Add green beans, and toss to coat. Saute until the beans are heated through.
6. Sprinkle with nuts and crumbled blue cheese.
7. Season with salt and pepper to taste.

Green Beans, Fennel, and Feta Cheese

Ingredients:

1 pound fresh green beans, trimmed
1 fennel bulb, cut into thin slices
1/4 cup extra-virgin olive oil
2 tbsps. chopped fresh basil leaves
Salt and pepper to taste
1/4 cup crumbled feta cheese

Directions:

1. Fill a saucepan half full with water and bring to a boil.
2. Add the green beans and fennel slices; cook until just beginning to become tender, about 4 minutes.
3. Pour into a colander to drain and run under cold water to stop the cooking process.
4. Return the empty pan to the stove and set heat to medium.
5. Pour in the olive oil and let it heat for a minute. Return the green beans and fennel to the pan.
6. Season with basil, salt, and pepper; cook and stir until coated and warm. Transfer to a serving dish and toss with feta cheese.

Sesame Green Beans

Ingredients:

1 tbsp. olive oil
1 tbsp. sesame seeds
1 pound fresh green beans, cut into 2 inch pieces
1/4 cup chicken broth
1/4 tsp. salt
Ground black pepper to taste

Directions:

1. Heat oil in a large skillet or wok over medium heat.
2. Add sesame seeds. When seeds start to darken, stir in green beans.
3. Cook, stirring, until the beans turn bright green.
4. Pour in chicken broth, salt and pepper.
5. Cover and cook until beans are tender-crisp, about 10 minutes. Uncover and cook until liquid evaporates.

Bok Choy, Carrots and Green Beans

Ingredients:

1 tsp. peanut oil
3 tbsps. minced shallots
2 carrots, sliced diagonally
1 cup fresh green beans, cut into 1 inch pieces
1 cup chopped bok choy
1/3 cup vegetable broth
1 tbsp. light soy sauce

Directions:

1. Heat the oil in a wok or skillet over high heat.
2. Add the shallots and saute for 3 minutes.
3. Add the carrots and stir fry for 3 minutes.
4. Add the green beans and stir fry for 2 minutes.
5. Add the bok choy and stir fry for 2 minutes.
6. Add the broth and simmer for 2 minutes.
7. Add the soy sauce and serve.

Beet Greens and Green Beans

Ingredients:

2 tbsps. olive oil
1/2 small yellow onion, chopped
1 cup fresh green beans, trimmed
2 cups chopped beet greens
1 small tomato, chopped
1 large clove garlic, minced
1/4 tsp. ground thyme
1/8 tsp. red pepper flakes
1/4 cup water
2 tbsps. cider vinegar
Sea salt to taste
Ground black pepper to taste

Directions:

1. Heat olive oil in a large skillet over medium heat; cook and stir onion in hot oil until browned, about 10 minutes.
2. Cook and stir green beans with onion until lightly brown.
3. Add beet greens, tomato, and garlic. Continue cooking until beet greens are wilted.
4. Sprinkle thyme and red pepper flakes over vegetables.
5. Stir in water, vinegar, salt, and pepper.

Grecian Green Beans in Tomato Sauce

Ingredients:

2 pounds fresh green beans, trimmed
6 tbsps. lemon juice
1 medium onion, chopped
3/4 cup olive oil
1 (16 oz.) can diced tomatoes
1 (8 oz.) can tomato sauce
2 tbsps. dried parsley
1 cup water
2 pounds fresh green beans, trimmed
6 tbsps. lemon juice
1 medium onion, chopped
3/4 cup olive oil
1 (16 oz.) can diced tomatoes
1 (8 oz.) can tomato sauce
2 tbsps. dried parsley
1 cup water
salt and pepper to taste1 bay leaf

Directions:

1. Place the green beans in a pot, and mix in the lemon juice, onion, olive oil, tomatoes, tomato sauce, parsley, water, salt and pepper, and bay leaf.
2. Cook 45 minutes over medium heat, stirring occasionally, until sauce is thickened.
3. Remove bay leaf before serving.

Green Beans with Mustard Cream Sauce

Ingredients:

4 tbsp. butter
1 (16 oz.) package frozen pear
1 onion
2 pound green beans, trimmed and snapped into 2-inch pieces
1 1/2 cup milk
1/2 cup chicken broth
1/4 cup Dijon mustard
3 tbsp. flour
1/2 cup slivered almonds, toasted until fragrant in a 325 degree F oven (10 minutes or less)

Directions:

1. Heat 2 tbsps. of butter in a large, deep skillet over medium-high heat.
2. Add onions; saute, shaking pan occasionally, until golden brown, 5 to 7 minutes.
3. Dump onions onto a large cookie sheet.
4. Add green beans, 3/4 cup water and a scant tsp. salt to the unwashed skillet. Turn heat to high; cover and cook until wisps of steam escape around the lid. Set timer for 5 minutes; cook until bright green but tender.
5. Drain beans; transfer to cookie sheet with onions and spread out to cool. (Cooled vegetables can be covered loosely with plastic wrap and set aside at room temperature up to 4 hours ahead.)
6. Microwave milk, chicken broth and mustard in a 1-quart Pyrex-type measuring cup until steamy. Heat remaining 2 Tbs. of butter in the skillet. Whisk in flour, then hot milk mixture, until smooth and simmering. (Sauce can be made up to 4 hours ahead: Cover surface directly with plastic wrap, to prevent a skin from forming, and refrigerate; return to a simmer before proceeding.)
7. Add beans and onions; simmer until sauce is thick enough to cling, about 5 minutes.
8. Season with salt and pepper to taste. Transfer to a serving bowl, sprinkle with toasted almonds and serve immediately.

Russian Green Bean and Potato Soup

Ingredients:

1 tbsp. vegetable oil
1 large onion, halved and thinly sliced
4 red potatoes, cubed
1/2 pound green beans, cut into 1 inch pieces
5 cups vegetable, chicken, or beef broth
2 tbsps. whole wheat flour
1/2 cup sour cream
3/4 cup sauerkraut with juice
1 tbsp. chopped fresh dill
Salt and pepper to taste

Directions:

1. Heat vegetable oil in a large saucepan over medium heat.
2. Stir in the onion, and gently cook until softened and translucent, about 5 minutes.
3. Add the potatoes and green beans; cook until the green beans have slightly softened, about 5 more minutes.
4. Pour in the vegetable stock.
5. Bring to a boil over high heat, then lower heat to medium-low, cover, and cook until the potatoes have softened, about 15 minutes.
6. Stir the flour into the sour cream, and add it a spoonful at a time to the simmering soup.
7. Stir in the sauerkraut and dill, season to taste with salt and pepper. Simmer for 5 minutes more before serving.

Cheesy Vegetable Chowder

Ingredients:

7 cups water
9 cubes chicken bouillon, crumbled
6 potatoes, cubed
2 cloves garlic, minced
1 large white onion, chopped
1 bunch celery, chopped
3 cups chopped carrots
2 (15 oz.) cans whole kernel corn
2 (15 oz.) cans peas
2 cups chopped fresh green beans
1/2 cup butter
1/2 cup all-purpose flour
3 cups milk
1 pound processed cheese, cubed
3 cups chopped carrots
2 (15 oz.) cans whole kernel corn
2 (15 oz.) cans peas
2 cups chopped fresh green beans
1/2 cup butter
1/2 cup all-purpose flour
3 cups milk
1 pound processed cheese, cubed

Directions:

1. In a large pot over medium heat, combine water, bouillon, potatoes and garlic.
2. Bring to a boil, then stir in onion, celery and carrots.
3. Reduce heat and simmer 15 minutes.
4. Stir in corn, peas and green beans and continue to cook on low heat.
5. Meanwhile, in a medium saucepan over medium heat, melt butter. Whisk in flour all at once to form a roux and let cook 10 seconds. Whisk in milk, a little at a time, and cook, stirring, until mixture is thick and bubbly.
6. Stir in cheese until melted.
7. Pour this mixture into the large soup pot, stir well and heat through.

Curried Green Bean Salad

Ingredients:

3 tbsps. minced fresh onion
1 tbsp. curry powder
1 tbsp. rice vinegar
2 tsps. minced fresh garlic
1 tsp. minced fresh ginger root
1/4 cup canola oil
Salt and ground black pepper to taste
2 (14.5 oz.) cans green beans, drained
1/2 cup slivered almonds

Directions:

1. Mix onion, curry powder, rice vinegar, garlic, and ginger together in a large bowl.
2. Stir oil into the onion mixture; season with salt and black pepper; mix well.
3. Add green beans and almonds to the mixture; toss lightly to coat.

Green Beans and Potato Salad

Ingredients:

1 pound bacon
3 pounds new red potatoes, quartered
1 pound fresh green beans, cut into bite-sized pieces
1 (16 fl oz) bottle balsamic vinaigrette salad dressing
3 roasted red peppers, diced
1 red onion, diced
1/2 tsp. salt
1/2 tsp. ground black pepper

Directions:

1. Cook bacon in a large skillet over medium-high heat until crisp, about 10 minutes.
2. Drain the bacon slices on paper towels; chop and set aside.
3. Place potatoes into a large pot and cover with salted water; bring to a boil.
4. Reduce heat to medium-low and simmer until tender, about 8 minutes.
5. Add green beans to the water.
6. Bring the water again to a boil and cook until the green beans are slightly tender, about 2 minutes; drain. Cool potatoes and green beans slightly before transferring to a serving bowl.
7. Mix balsamic vinaigrette, chopped bacon, red pepper, red onion, salt, and black pepper together in a bowl; pour over the potatoes and green beans.

Navratan Korma with Green Beans

Ingredients:

3 tbsps. vegetable oil, divided
1/3 cup mixed nuts (cashews, pistachios, almonds)
1 medium onion, grated
1/2 tsp. garlic paste
1/2 tsp. ginger paste
1 (8 oz.) can tomato sauce
1 tsp. cayenne pepper
1/2 tsp. ground turmeric
2 tsps. ground coriander
1 tsp. garam masala
1 cup water
1/4 cup raisins
1/2 cup chopped carrots
1/2 cup chopped green bell pepper
1/2 cup chopped fresh green beans
1/2 cup green peas
1 cup chopped potatoes
4 oz. paneer, cubed
1/4 cup milk
1/4 cup heavy cream
Salt to taste

Directions:

1. Heat 1 tbsp. oil in a large skillet over medium heat.
2. Place mixed nuts in the skillet, cook and stir until golden brown, and set aside.
3. Stir onion into the skillet, and cook until tender.
4. Mix in garlic paste and ginger paste, and cook 1 minute.
5. Stir in tomato sauce, cayenne pepper, turmeric, coriander, and garam masala.
6. Pour in water, and mix in raisins, carrots, green bell pepper, beans, peas, and potatoes.
7. Bring to a boil.
8. Reduce heat to low, and simmer 20 minutes, until potatoes are tender.
9. Heat remaining oil in a separate skillet over medium-high heat, and cook the paneer on both sides, until golden brown.
10. Drain on paper towels.
11. Place in a bowl with enough hot water to cover for about 2 minutes to soften, then stir into the skillet with the vegetables.
12. Stir milk and cream into the skillet with the vegetables and paneer.
13. Bring to a boil, and continue cooking 2 to 3 minutes.
14. Season with salt to taste.

Pesto Pasta with Potatoes and Green Beans

Ingredients:

1 pound cavatappi pasta
1/2 pound green beans
3 medium large red potatoes
3/4 cup basil pesto
Fresh Parmesan cheese, to serve

Directions:

1. Wash the green beans, remove the ends, and chop them into 2-inch pieces. Wash the potatoes and cut them into 1-inch chunks.
2. Place the potatoes in a pot and cover them with water.
3. Bring the potatoes to a boil and cook them until tender, about 10 minutes.
4. Drain and place in a large bowl.
5. Meanwhile, place water in another pot and bring to a boil. When it is boiling, add the green beans and cook until tender, around 6 minutes.
6. Remove the beans with a slotted spoon and place in the bowl with the potatoes.
7. Reserve the hot water from the green beans to use for the pasta, adding more to be able to cover the pasta when it is added.
8. Bring the water to a boil and add a pinch of salt.
9. Add the cavatappi and boil until tender according to the package instructions, around 8 minutes.
10. Drain and place in the bowl with the potatoes, reserving a bit of cooking water in the pot.
11. Add 3/4 cup pesto to the large bowl and mix everything to combine. You can add a bit of cooking water to help the mixing process, and season with salt and pepper to taste.
12. Serve topped with freshly grated Parmesan.

Chicken, Green Bean And Butternut Squash Curry

Ingredients:

1 tbsp. cooking oil
1 medium brown onion , chopped
1 medium carrot , peeled and diced
6 skinless chicken thigh fillets , cut into pieces
4 cloves garlic , crushed
3 tbsps. Thai red curry paste
4 cups ready diced butternut squash
1 cup green beans, trimmed
1 can coconut milk
1 tbsp. brown sugar
Salt to taste
Fresh coriander leaves to serve

Directions:

1. Heat the oil in a large pan/skillet on high heat. Sauté the onion and carrot until the onion becomes soft and transparent.
2. Add the chicken and fry until just beginning to brown.
3. Add the garlic and curry paste (if using), stirring together quickly to blend in the heat of the pan for about a minute until fragrant.
4. Add the butternut pieces and green beans; keep cooking while stirring occasionally for 5 minutes.
5. Stir the coconut milk through the ingredients and bring to a simmer.
6. Reduce heat to low; add in the sugar and salt to your taste (I use about 1 tsp.), and continue to simmer for about 10-15 minutes, or until the pumpkin pieces have softened. (If you prefer a creamier pumpkin curry sauce, simmer for 5-10 minutes longer until the pumpkin has completely melted through the sauce. YUM.
7. Serve over steamed rice or cauliflower rice.

Green Bean Salad with Peaches and Vinaigrette

Ingredients:

4 cups thinly sliced purple cabbage
Sea salt
2 cups green beans, stem end snapped off
1 large or 2 small spring onions , thinly sliced plus 1 tbsp., minced
2 jalapeños , seeded and thinly sliced plus 1 tsp., minced
1 clove garlic , smashed and minced
3 tbsps. balsamic vinegar
1 drizzle of aged balsamic vinegar
3 tbsps. extra virgin olive oil
1/2 tsp. whiskey barrel-aged bitters
2 peaches , cut into 1/8-inch slices
2 tbsps. torn basil leaves
Black pepper

Directions:

1. Set the sliced cabbage in a colander, and sprinkle with 1/2 tsp. of sea salt. Set aside to drain for 20 minutes or more, turning every so often to release juices.
2. Next, bring a large pot of cold water to a rapid boil.
3. Add a generous amount of sea salt. Blanch the green beans until vibrant green and just tender (2 - 3 minutes, depending on the size).
4. Drain, immerse cooked green beans in ice water, and drain again.
5. Slice each cooked green bean in half lengthwise.
6. To make the balsamic and bitters vinaigrette, combine 1 tbsp. minced spring onion, 1 tsp. minced jalapeño, 1 clove garlic, and a pinch of sea salt. Use a fork to whisk in the balsamic vinegar. Whisking constantly, drizzle in the olive oil until emulsified. Finish by whisking in the bitters.
7. Set the sliced cabbage in a bowl with remaining spring onion and jalapeño slices.
8. Toss with a third of the vinaigrette.
9. In another bowl, toss the halved green beans with a third of the vinaigrette and several pinches of sea salt, as needed. Allow vegetables and vinaigrette to mingle for 10 minutes.
10. To assemble the salad, toss the dressed cabbage and green bean mixtures with sliced peaches, torn basil leaves, and the remaining third of the vinaigrette. If using an aged balsamic vinegar, add a generous drizzle to the salad. Finish with ground black pepper to taste.
11. Salad will keep well sealed in the fridge for 2 days, though the colors and textures are most vibrant just after assembly.

Lebanese Green Bean Stew (Loubieh)

Ingredients:

2 tbsps. olive oil
1 medium onion, diced
5 garlic cloves, minced
1 1/2 cups vegetable broth
1 14 oz. can diced tomatoes
2 tbsps. tomato paste
12 oz. fresh green beans, cut into 2 inch pieces
1 cup cooked or canned chickpeas, drained and rinsed
1/2 cup slivered almonds
1 tsp. ground cumin
Salt and pepper to taste
Fresh parsley, for serving

Directions:

1. Coat the bottom of a medium pot with oil and place it over medium-low heat.
2. Add the onion and cook for about 25 to 30 minutes, flipping occasionally, until the onion begins to caramelize.
3. Add the garlic and cook about 1 minute more, until very fragrant.
4. Add the broth, diced tomatoes, tomato paste, green beans, chickpeas, almonds, and cumin to the pot and give everything a stir. Raise the heat to high and bring to a simmer. Lower heat and allow to simmer until the base has thickened up and the beans are tender, 20 to 30 minutes depending on how soft you like your veggies.
5. Remove from heat and season with salt and pepper to taste. Divide into bowls and garnish with parsley. Serve.

Thai Green Beans

Ingredients:

For the green beans:
1/2 tbsp. toasted sesame oil
2 cloves garlic, thinly sliced
1 pound green beans, rinsed and ends trimmed
For the sauce:
1 tbsp. reduced sodium soy sauce or coconut aminos
1/2 tbsp. toasted sesame oil
2 tbsps. creamy peanut butter
1 tsp. freshly grated ginger
1 tsp. rice wine vinegar
1/4 tsp. red pepper flakes
1/4 cup water
Salt, to taste
To garnish: Green onion, sesame seeds and a tbsp. or two of cashews/roasted peanuts

Directions:

1. Place a large skillet over medium heat.
2. Add in 1/2 tbsp. sesame oil and garlic, saute for 30 seconds or until garlic is fragrant. Immediately add in green beans; stir frequently until beans are slightly golden brown, about 5-8 minutes.
3. While the beans are cooking, make the sauce: In a medium bowl, add soy sauce, sesame oil, peanut butter, ginger, vinegar, red pepper flakes and water.
4. Stir to combine.
5. One green beans are cooked and slightly golden and al dente, reduce heat to low and pour sauce over the beans.
6. Stir to coat the beans, then cover and simmer for a few minutes to allow the beans to continue cooking.
7. Taste and add salt, if necessary. Garnish with sliced green onion, sesame seeds and a tbsp. or two of cashews.

Green Bean Artichoke Casserole

Ingredients:

3 (15.5 oz.) cans French cut green beans, drained
2 (14 oz.) cans artichoke hearts, drained
2 cups Italian seasoned bread crumbs
8 oz. grated Parmesan cheese
8 oz. shredded mozzarella cheese
2 tbsps. garlic powder
Salt and pepper to taste1/
2 cup olive oil

Directions:

1. Preheat the oven to 400 degrees F (200 degrees C).
2. Pour the green beans, artichoke hearts, bread crumbs, Parmesan cheese, and mozzarella cheese into a 9x13 inch baking dish.
3. Season with garlic powder, salt and pepper.
4. Stir to blend everything thoroughly. Drizzle olive oil over the top, then cover the dish with aluminum foil.
5. Bake for 30 minutes in the preheated oven, then remove the aluminum foil, and bake for another 15 minutes to brown the top slightly.

Green Bean Mushroom Tart

Ingredients:

1 sheet of thawed puff pastry
1 large egg
3/4 pound thin green beans, trimmed
3 tbsps. butter, divided
8 oz. cremini mushrooms, sliced thin
1 clove garlic, minced
4 sprigs fresh thyme
2 shallots, peeled and sliced thin
2 oz. crumbled blue cheese
Salt and pepper

Directions:

1. Preheat the oven to 425 degrees F. Line a cookie sheet with parchment paper and set aside.
2. Blanch the green beans in boiling water for 1-2 minutes.
3. Drain and place in cold water to cool. Then set on a paper towel to dry.
4. Melt 2 tbsps. of butter in a skillet over medium heat.
5. Add the mushrooms and the thyme and saute for 3-5 minutes. Then add the garlic, and salt and pepper to taste. Saute another 2-3 minutes and remove from skillet and pull out the thyme sprigs.
6. Add the remaining butter to the skillet with the sliced shallots. Saute until golden-brown and crispy, 5-8 minutes.
7. Meanwhile, cut the puff pastry down the middle and place both pieces 3-4 inches apart on the cookie sheet. Whisk the egg with a tbsp. of water, and brush the pastry sheets with egg. Neatly layer green beans down the length of each puff pastry rectangle.
8. On both puff pastry sheets, top the green beans with mushrooms, crumbled blue cheese, and crispy onions. Salt and Pepper lightly.
9. Bake for 15-20 minutes until the edges are golden. Serve warm or room temperature.

Sheet Pan Mongolian Beef

Ingredients:

1 pound green beans, trimmed and halved
1 pound flank steak
1/4 cup corn starch
5 tbsps. coconut oil, divided
1 tbsps. fresh grated ginger
6 cloves garlic, minced
1/3 cup low sodium soy sauce
1/3 cup brown sugar
3 tbsps. sherry
1 tsp. crushed red pepper
1/2 cup chopped scallions

Directions:

1. Preheat the oven to 450 degrees F, convection if possible.
2. Slice the flank steak against the grain, into thin slivers. Then toss the strips with cornstarch.
3. Spread the green beans out on a large rimmed baking sheet and drizzle with 3 tbsps. melted coconut oil.
4. Sprinkle with pepper. Roast the green beans for 5 minutes.
5. Move the green beans to the sides of the pan, and spread the flank steak slivers across the center in a single layer. Drizzle the steak with 2 tbsps. coconut oil and roast in the oven for 8 minutes.
6. Meanwhile, whisk the ginger, garlic, soy sauce, brown sugar, sherry and crushed red pepper together.
7. Remove the sheet pan from the oven.
8. Pour the sauce over the top of the steak. Roast again for 7 minutes. Then toss the beef and beans together and sprinkle with chopped scallions.

Southwest Brussels and Beans

Ingredients:

1 pound brussels spouts, trimmed and halved
1/2 pound french green beans, trimmed
3 tbsps. olive oil
1 1/2 tbsps. taco Seasoning
1 cup shredded cheese (colby, cheddar, or monterey jack)
1/2 cup chopped green onions

Directions:

1. Preheat the oven to 400 degrees F. Line a large rimmed baking sheet with parchment paper. Then place the cut brussels sprouts and french beans on top.
2. Drizzle 3 tbsps. olive oil over the top of the veggies, then sprinkle with Old El Paso Taco Seasoning.
3. Toss to coat and spread out evenly in a single layer.
4. Roast in the oven for 20-25 minutes, until the brussels sprouts are cooked but firm. Then sprinkle cheese over the top and place back in the oven for 2-3 minutes to melt the cheese. Once out of the oven, sprinkle fresh chopped green onions over the top and serve immediately.

Grilled Chicken Rasta Pasta

Ingredients:

1 1/2 pounds boneless skinless chicken
1 1/4 tsps. curry powder
1 1/4 tsps. sea salt
1/2 tsp. ground allspice
1/2 tsp. dried thyme
1/4 tsp. garlic powder
1 large red bell pepper seeded and cut into long strips
1/2 red onion peeled and cut intoÂ wedges

Pasta Ingredients:

1 pound rolled bucatini pasta or penne
8 oz. green beans trimmed
1 tbsp. butter
3 garlic cloves minced
1 habanero pepper seeded and minced
1/3 cup heavy cream
2 tsps. powdered chicken boullion
2 cups shredded Mexican blend cheese
1 1/2 cups reserved pasta water

Directions:

1. Preheat the grill (or a) to medium heat.
2. Mix the curry powder, salt, allspice, thyme, and garlic powder together in a small bowl. Rub the spice blend over the chicken, covering all sides. Once the grill is hot, grill the chicken for 5 minutes per side. Lay the onion wedges and peppers carefully across the grates and grill 2 minutes per side.
3. Meanwhile, fill a large deep sauté pan with water and place on the stovetop over high heat. Once boiling, add 1 tbsp. salt and the pasta.
4. Stir to separate the pasta, then cook according to package instructions, usually 6-8 minutes to . When the pasta only has 1 minute left to cook, add in the green beans to blanche for the last minute.
5. Drain the pasta and beans, . Rinse the pasta and beans in cold water and shake well.
6. Once the chicken has cooled for at least 5 minutes, slice into strips. Then cut the chicken strips in smaller bite size pieces.
7. Cut the grilled pepper strips in half to create shorter segments.
8. Place the butter, minced garlic, and habanero in the large sauté pan. Sauté over medium heat for 1-2 minutes. Then add the heavy cream, chicken bouillon, pasta, green beans, 1 cup reserved pasta water, and Borden®Cheese Shreds.
9. Stir to coat and melt the cheese.

10. Mix in the grilled chicken, onions, and peppers. Continue to stir until the liquid and cheese form a creamy sauce.
11. Stir in the remaining pasta water if the sauce is too thick. Serve warm.

Green Beans with Caramelized Onions

Ingredients:

1 tbsp. olive oil
1 tbsp. white sugar
1 (16 oz.) package frozen pearl onions
1 (16 oz.) package frozen cut green beans, thawed
1 tbsp. fresh dill weed
1/2 tsp. salt
1/4 tsp. ground black pepper

Directions:

1. Heat the oil and sugar in a large skillet over medium-high heat.
2. Add the onions; cook and stir until tender and golden brown, about 10 minutes.
3. Mix the green beans with the onions, and cook for about 3 minutes.
4. Remove from heat and season with dill, salt and pepper.

Swiss Green Beans

Ingredients:

5 tbsps. butter, melted
2 tbsps. all-purpose flour
2 tsps. grated onion
1 tsp. white sugar
1 tsp. salt (optional)
1/4 tsp. ground black pepper, or to taste
1 cup sour cream
8 oz. Swiss cheese, grated
2 (15 oz.) cans cut green beans, drained
1 cup cornflakes cereal crumbs

Directions:

1. Preheat oven to 400 degrees F (200 degrees C).
2. In a 3 quart saucepan combine 2 tbsps. melted butter, flour, onion, sugar, salt, pepper, sour cream and 4 oz. of the cheese.
3. Cook over low heat and stir constantly until thickened.
4. Fold in green beans.
5. Pour into a 2 quart casserole dish and sprinkle the rest of the cheese on top.
6. In a small bowl combine cereal crumbs and melted butter; sprinkle over beans.
7. Bake in preheated oven for 20 minutes.

Creole Green Beans

Ingredients:

1/4 cup unsalted butter
1 (14 oz.) package frozen green beans
6 thick slices bacon, chopped
1/2 onion, chopped
1/2 green bell pepper, chopped
2 cloves garlic, chopped
1 tsp. cayenne pepper
1 tsp. Creole seasoning
1/4 tsp. ground black pepper
Salt to taste

Directions:

1. Melt butter over medium heat in a large skillet.
2. Stir in green beans, bacon, onion, green pepper, and garlic; cook and stir until onions are translucent, about 2 minutes.
3. Stir in cayenne pepper, Creole seasoning, and black pepper.
4. Cover; reduce heat to low.
5. Simmer until vegetables are tender, about 20 minutes.
6. Season to taste with salt.

Squash and Green Bean Saute

Ingredients:

2 yellow squash, sliced
1 1/2 cups green beans
1 1/2 cups halved cherry tomatoes
2 tbsps. fresh lemon juice
1 tbsp. dried parsley
1/2 tsp. ground coriander
1/8 tsp. salt, or to taste
1/8 tsp. ground black pepper, or to taste

Directions:

1. Cook and stir squash and green beans in a nonstick skillet over medium heat until slightly softened, 2 to 3 minutes.
2. Stir tomatoes, lemon juice, parsley, coriander, salt, and black pepper into squash mixture; cook and stir until tomatoes have softened, 5 to 10 minutes.

Fresh Oregano and Blackberry Green Beans

Ingredients:

2 pounds fresh green beans, cut into 2 inch pieces
2 tbsps. chopped fresh oregano
1/4 tsp. celery salt
1/2 tsp. onion powder
1/2 pint fresh, blackberries
Salt and pepper to taste

Directions:

1. Fill a saucepan with 1 inch of water, and insert a steamer basket.
2. Place the green beans into the steamer basket, and sprinkle with oregano, celery salt, and onion powder.
3. Cover and bring to a boil over high heat. Steam for 5 minutes, then remove beans from steamer basket, and place into a large bowl.
4. Gently fold in the blackberries, allowing the heat from the green beans to pull out their juices.
5. Season to taste with salt and pepper, and serve.

Green Beans with Feta and Walnuts

Ingredients:

1 tbsp. extra-virgin olive oil
1 tsp. chopped garlic
1/4 cup chopped walnuts
1 pound fresh green beans, trimmed
3 tbsps. crumbled feta cheese

Directions:

1. Heat olive oil in a skillet over medium heat; add garlic and cook and stir until fragrant, about 2 minutes.
2. Add walnuts to skillet, cook and stir until lightly toasted, about 2 minutes; stir in green beans, toss lightly to coat, and cook and stir until warmed through, 2 to 3 minutes.
3. Transfer green beans to serving bowl and immediately top with crumbled feta cheese.

Sriracha Green Beans

Ingredients:

Kosher salt
1 pound green beans, trimmed
2 tbsps. fresh lime juice
1 tbsp. packed brown sugar
3 tsps. Sriracha sauce
1 tbsp. vegetable oil
1/4 cup chopped fresh cilantro
4 tsps. toasted sesame seeds
Coarse salt

Directions:

1. Bring a large pot of water to boil over high heat.
2. Season generously with salt (it should taste like sea water), add green beans and cook until just tender, 5 to 8 minutes.
3. Drain, cool under cold running water and blot dry on kitchen towel.
4. Whisk together 4 tsps. of lime juice, brown sugar, and sriracha sauce in small bowl. Heat oil in large skillet set over medium-high heat until smoking.
5. Add green beans and toss to coat with oil.
6. Stirring very little, cook until beans are browned in spots and tender, about 5 minutes.
7. Add lime juice mixture, toss beans to coat and cook until moisture is evaporated, about 1 minute. Off heat, add cilantro, sesame seeds and remaining lime juice; toss. Serve immediately sprinkled with coarse salt.

Bloody Mary Green Beans

Ingredients:

3/4 pound green beans
1 small chili pepper, fresh or dried
1 clove garlic, peeled and slightly crushed
1-2 sprigs fresh thyme
1 tsp. celery seeds
1 tsp. whole mustard seeds
4 black peppercorns
2/3 cup white wine (or apple cider vinegar)
1/3 cup water
3 tsps. hot sauce

Directions:

1. Trim the beans to no more than 4 inches long.
2. Add the celery and mustard seeds and the black peppercorns to a clean (no need to sterilize for this recipe) pint-sized canning jar. Turn the canning jar onto its side.
3. Start filling the jar with the beans, laying them in so that they will be vertical when the jar is upright.
4. Add the garlic, chile pepper, and fresh thyme sprigs as you go. I like to place these right up against the jar's glass sides so that they can be seen.
5. Keep adding beans until they are tightly packed together.
6. They will shrink somewhat during the canning process, and if they are too loosely packed, they will float up above the brine. You don't want that to happen so pack them in really tightly. You can use a few shorter pieces of beans to wedge in the longer pieces.
7. Bring the vinegar, water, hot sauce and salt to a boil in a small pot.
8. Pour over the beans so the beans are completely immersed in the brine, but al at least 1/2-inch headspace between the top of the food and the rim of the jar.
9. Wipe the rim of the jar with a clean, moistened cloth or paper towel (any liquid on the rim could prevent a good seal).
10. Screw on the 2-piece canning lid(s). Store in the refrigerator for up to 2 months. For longer storage at room temperature, process in a boiling water bath for 10 minutes.
11. Wait at least 4 days for the flavors to develop before serving.

Spicy Pickled Green Beans

Ingredients:

2 cups white vinegar
3 tbsps. kosher salt
1 1/2 tbsps. sugar
3 tbsps. thinly sliced garlic (about 8 cloves)
8 fresh dill sprigs
4 small dried hot red chilis
1 1/2 pounds green beans, trimmed

Directions:

1. Combine first 4 ingredients in a large saucepan; bring to a boil.
2. Remove from heat; add garlic, dill, and peppers to pan.
3. Let stand 1 minute.
4. Pour vinegar mixture over beans in a large glass bowl; cover and refrigerate 1 week, stirring occasionally.

Dilly Green Beans

Ingredients:

6 cups water
1 cup pickling salt
6 cups distilled white vinegar
8 heads fresh dill weed
1/2 cup pickling spice
1/2 cup mustard seed
8 dried red chili peppers
16 cloves garlic, peeled
1 tsp. alum
5 pounds fresh green beans, rinsed and trimmed

Directions:

1. Sterilize 8 (1 pint) jars in boiling water for at least 5 minutes.
2. Combine the water, pickling salt and vinegar in a large pot, and bring to a boil. When it begins to boil, reduce heat to low, and keep at a simmer while you pack the jars.
3. In each jar place the following: 1 head of dill, 1 tbsp. of pickling spice, 1 tbsp. of mustard seed, 1 dried chili pepper, 2 cloves of garlic, and 1/8 tsp. of alum. Pack beans into the spiced jars in a standing position.
4. Ladle the hot brine into jars, leaving 1/2 inch of space at the top. Screw the lids onto the jars, and process in a hot water bath for 6 minutes to seal. Store for at least 2 weeks before eating.

Slow Cooker Green Beans, Ham and Potatoes

Ingredients:

2 pounds fresh green beans, rinsed and trimmed
1 large onion, chopped
3 ham hocks
1 1/2 pounds new potatoes, quartered
1 tsp. garlic powder
1 tsp. onion powder
1 tsp. seasoning salt
1 tbsp. chicken bouillon granules
Ground black pepper to taste

Directions:

1. Halve beans if they are large, place in a slow cooker with water to barely cover, and add onion and ham hocks.
2. Cover, and cook on High until simmering.
3. Reduce heat to Low, and cook for 2 to 3 hours, or until beans are crisp but not done.
4. Add potatoes, and cook for another 45 minutes. While potatoes are cooking, remove ham hocks from slow cooker, and remove meat from bones. Chop or shred meat, and return to slow cooker.
5. Season with garlic powder, onion powder, seasoning salt, bouillon, and pepper.
6. Cook until potatoes are done, then adjust seasoning to taste.
7. To serve, use a slotted spoon to put beans, potatoes, and ham into a serving dish with a little broth.

Green Bean with Tabasco Vinaigrette

Salad Ingredients:

1/2 lb. fresh green beans, trimmed and cut into 2-inch pieces
1/2 lb. fresh wax beans, trimmed and cut into 2-inch pieces
5 oz. greens
1/2 cup red onion, cut into crescents
4 slices pepper bacon, crisply cooked, drained

Vinaigrette Ingredients:

1/3 cup extra virgin olive oil
1/4 cup green Tabasco jalapeno sauce
1 garlic clove, peeled and minced finely
1/4 tsp. salt

Directions:

1. Cook the beans in a large pot of rapidly boiling salted water for approximately 10 minutes, or until crisp-tender.
2. In a large non-reactive bowl combine the vinaigrette ingredients and whisk.
3. Drain the beans, place in a large non-reactive bowl and toss them with the vinaigrette. Allow mixture to marinate for 30 minutes at room temperature.
4. On a large platter arrange the lettuce greens. Spoon the beans on the lettuce greens.
5. Arrange the red onion crescents on top of the beans.
6. Crumble the cooked bacon and garnish on top of the salad.

Haricots Verts With Sauce Ravigote

Ingredients:

1 pound green beans, trimmed
1/4 tsp. salt
2 tbsps. red wine vinegar
1/2 tsp. Dijon mustard
2 tsps. minced shallots
6 tbsps. extra virgin olive oil
2 tbsps. capers
2 tbsps. minced parsley
Salt and pepper to taste

Directions:

1. Put green beans and 1/4 tsp. salt in a large saute pan. Just barely cover beans with cold water. Turn heat to medium and cook beans until crisp tender, about 3 minutes.
2. Drain beans.
3. In a small bowl, whisk together mustard, vinegar, and shallots. Whisk in olive oil until emulsified.
4. Stir in capers and parsley.
5. Place green beans in a serving bowl.
6. Toss gently with vinaigrette.
7. Season with salt and pepper to taste.

Green Bean Salad with Anchovy Dressing

Ingredients:

Kosher salt
2 1/4 pounds green beans, trimmed
1/2 cup mayonnaise
6 whole anchovy filets, chopped into a paste
1 cup finely grated parmesan cheese
2 tbsps. fresh juice from 1 lemon
2 tsps. Worcestershire sauce
Freshly ground black pepper
1/2 cup sliced Pepperoncini, drained
2 medium shallots, finely sliced (about 2/3 cup)
1/4 cup toasted pine nuts

Directions:

1. Bring a large pot of salted water to a boil over high heat. Fill a large bowl with water and ice.
2. Add beans to boiling water and cook until tender crisp, about 4 minutes. Transfer to ice bath until cool. Transfer to a rimmed baking sheet lined with paper towels or a clean kitchen towel and dry beans carefully (see note). Set aside.
3. Combine mayonnaise, anchovies, parmesan, lemon juice, and Worcestershire sauce in a large bowl and whisk to combine.
4. Season to taste with salt and pepper.
5. Add beans, pepperoncini, shallots, and pine nuts.
6. Toss to combine, and serve.

Minestrone

Ingredients:

3 tbsps. olive oil
3 cloves garlic, chopped
2 onions, chopped
2 cups chopped celery
5 carrots, sliced
2 cups chicken broth
2 cups water
4 cups tomato sauce
1/2 cup red wine (optional)
1 cup canned kidney beans, drained
1 (15 oz.) can green beans
2 cups baby spinach, rinsed
3 zucchinis, quartered and sliced
1 tbsp. chopped fresh oregano
2 tbsps. chopped fresh basil
Salt and pepper to taste
1/2 cup seashell pasta
2 tbsps. grated Parmesan cheese for topping
1 tbsp. olive oil

Directions:

1. In a large stock pot, over medium-low heat, heat olive oil and saute garlic for 2 to 3 minutes.
2. Add onion and saute for 4 to 5 minutes.
3. Add celery and carrots, saute for 1 to 2 minutes.
4. Add chicken broth, water and tomato sauce, bring to boil, stirring frequently. If desired add red wine at this point.
5. Reduce heat to low and add kidney beans, green beans, spinach leaves, zucchini, oregano, basil, salt and pepper. Simmer for 30 to 40 minutes, the longer the better.
6. Fill a medium saucepan with water and bring to a boil.
7. Add macaroni and cook until tender.
8. Drain water and set aside.
9. Once pasta is cooked and soup is heated through place 2 tbsps. cooked pasta into individual serving bowls. Ladle soup on top of pasta and sprinkle Parmesan cheese on top. Spray with olive oil and serve.

Cabbage Soup

Ingredients:

5 carrots, chopped
3 onions, chopped
2 (16 oz.) cans whole peeled tomatoes, with liquid
1 large head cabbage, chopped
1 (1 oz.) envelope dry onion soup mix
1 (15 oz.) can cut green beans, drained
2 quarts tomato juice
2 green bell peppers, diced
10 stalks celery, chopped
1 (14 oz.) can beef broth

Directions:

1. Place carrots, onions, tomatoes, cabbage, green beans, peppers, and celery in a large pot.
2. Add onion soup mix, tomato juice, beef broth, and enough water to cover vegetables. Simmer until vegetables are tender. May be stored in the refrigerator for several days.

Green Beans and Tomatoes

Ingredients:

1 tbsp. olive oil
1 1/2 pounds lamb stew meat
1 large onion, chopped
2 pounds fresh green beans, washed and trimmed
1 (15 oz.) can tomato sauce
1 cup water
Salt and pepper to taste
2 tsps. chopped fresh mint leaves

Directions:

1. Heat oil in a large skillet over medium high heat.
2. Add lamb and onion and cook until meat is browned; stir in beans and cook for about 10 minutes, stirring occasionally.
3. Stir in tomato sauce, water, salt, pepper and mint.
4. Reduce heat to low, cover and simmer for about 1 hour or until cooked through and beans are tender.

Grilled Sausage with Potatoes and Green Beans

Ingredients:

3/4 pound fresh green beans, trimmed and halved
1/2 pound red potatoes, quartered
1 large onion, sliced
1 pound smoked sausage, cut into 1 inch pieces
1 tsp. salt
1 tsp. ground black pepper
1 tsp. vegetable oil
1 tsp. butter
1/3 cup water

Directions:

1. Preheat an outdoor grill for high heat.
2. On a large sheet of foil, place the green beans, red potatoes, onion, and sausage.
3. Season with salt and pepper, sprinkle with oil, and top with butter. Tightly seal foil around the ingredients, leaving only a small opening.
4. Pour water into the opening, and seal.
5. Place foil packet on the prepared grill.
6. Cook 20 to 30 minutes, turning once, until sausage is browned and vegetables are tender.

Spinach Green Bean Casserole

Ingredients:

3/4 cup milk
1 cup sour cream
1 (10.75 oz.) can condensed cream of mushroom soup
2 (15 oz.) cans green beans, drained
1 (14 oz.) can chopped spinach, drained
2 (2.8 oz.) cans French fried onions

Directions:

1. Preheat the oven to 375 degrees F (190 degrees C)
2. Lightly grease a casserole dish.
3. Stir the milk, sour cream and cream of mushroom soup together in a large bowl.
4. Fold in the green beans and spinach, and mix in about half of the onions.
5. Pour into the casserole dish and top with the remaining onions.
6. Bake uncovered in the preheated oven until bubbly and browned on top, about 40 minutes.

Green Bean Wraps

Ingredients:

1 cup minced green beans
1/2 cup chopped green onions
1/2 cup bread crumbs
1/4 cup grated Parmesan cheese
2 tsps. garlic powder
2 tsps. Italian seasoning
1 tsp. dried basil
1 tsp. dried oregano
1/2 tsp. salt
1/4 tsp. ground black pepper
1/4 cup olive oil, or more as needed
8 slices provolone cheese
4 small flour tortillas

Directions:

1. Combine beans, green onions, bread crumbs, and Parmesan cheese in a bowl.
2. Add garlic powder, Italian seasoning, basil, oregano, salt, and black pepper and mix well.
3. Mix olive oil into bean mixture until desired moistness is reached.
4. Place 2 slices Provolone cheese onto each tortilla. Spoon bean mixture on top of cheese layer.
5. Wrap tortilla around the filling, starting from the bottom.

French Green Bean Stuffing

Ingredients:

1 cup butter
3/4 (16 oz.) package frozen French cut green beans
2 onions, chopped
2 leeks, chopped
1 tbsp. garlic and herb seasoning blend
2 eggs, lightly beaten
1 (16 oz.) package seasoned stuffing mix
2 cups hot water

Directions:

1.   Preheat oven to 375 degrees F (190 degrees C).
2.   Lightly grease a medium baking dish.
3.   In a skillet over medium heat, melt 2 tbsps. butter, and saute the green beans, onions, and leeks until tender.
4.   Season with garlic and herb seasoning blend.
5.   Mix in the remaining butter until melted.
6.   In a large bowl, toss together the green bean mixture, eggs, and dry stuffing mix.
7.   Gradually blend in the water. Transfer the mixture to the prepared baking dish.
8.   Bake 40 minutes in the preheated oven, or until lightly brown.

Coconut Chicken with Green Beans

Ingredients:

1 tbsp. oil
6-8 skinless and boneless chicken thighs
salt and pepper
1 onion chopped
1 tbsp ginger minced
3 cloves garlic minced
2 tbsp cumin
3 cardamom pods slightly crushed (optional)
1 tsp chipotle paste
1 1/2 tsp fish sauce
1 1/2 cups rice
2 tsp salt
1 3/4 cup water
1 (14 oz.) can coconut milk
1 cup green beans cut in half
Fresh chopped cilantro/coriander
Unsweetened dessicated coconut optional

Directions:

1. Preheat the oven to 350 degrees F (180 degrees C).
2. Season the chicken thighs with salt and pepper.
3. In a large pan heat the oil and brown the chicken thighs on high heat on each side until golden but not cooked all the way through, then remove to a plate.
4. Lower the heat and add onion and ginger, cook for 5 minutes, then add garlic, cumin, cardamom pods and chipotle paste, cook while scraping the bottom of the pan and stirring the whole time for 1 minutes.
5. Add rice and cook while stirring for 2 minutes, then add water, coconut milk, fish sauce and salt, stir to combine, turn up the heat and bring to a boil.
6. Return the chicken to the pot, add the green beans, cover with a lid and put in the oven for 20 minutes or until the rice is done.
7. By the end of the cooking time the liquid should be completely absorbed, producing light and fluffy rice.
8. Serve sprinkled with chopped cilantro/coriander and a handful of unsweetened coconut flakes if desired.

Green Bean Okazu

Ingredients:

1 pound ground beef
1 pound green beans, trimmed and cut into 1 inch pieces
1 cup water
1/4 cup white sugar
1/4 cup soy sauce

Directions:

1. In a large skillet over medium heat, cook the ground beef until evenly brown; drain excess fat.
2. Stir in green beans and about 1 cup water.
3. Cover, and cook until beans are tender, 15 to 20 minutes.
4. Season with sugar and soy sauce, and cook uncovered for 5 minutes.

About the Author

Laura Sommers is **The Recipe Lady!**

She is a loving wife and mother who lives on a small farm in Baltimore County, Maryland and has a passion for all things domestic especially when it comes to saving money. She has a profitable eBay business and is a couponing addict. Follow her tips and tricks to learn how to make delicious meals on a budget, save money or to learn the latest life hack!

Visit the Recipe Lady's blog for even more great recipes:

http://the-recipe-lady.blogspot.com/

Follow the Recipe Lady on **Pinterest**:

http://pinterest.com/therecipelady1

Please Leave a Review

If you enjoyed this book, please leave a review. Even one review can make the difference in the sales of these books which helps me to support my family. Even if you downloaded this book during a promotional period, a review will always help. Thank you very much!

Other Books by Laura Sommers

- Recipe Hacks for Beer
- Recipe Hacks for Potato Chips
- Recipe Hacks for a Bottle of Italian Salad Dressing
- Recipe Hacks for Dry Onion Soup Mix
- Recipe Hacks for Cheese Puffs
- Recipe Hacks for Pasta Sauce
- Recipe Hacks for Dry Vegetable Soup Mix
- Recipe Hacks for Canned Tuna Fish
- Recipe Hacks for Saltine Crackers
- Recipe Hacks for Pancake Mix
- Recipe Hacks for Instant Mashed Potato Flakes
- Recipe Hacks for Sriracha Hot Chili Sauce
- Recipe Hacks for Dry Ranch Salad Dressing and Dip Mix
- Recipe Hacks for Canned Biscuits
- Recipe Hacks for Canned Soup
- Recipe Hacks for Oreo Cookies
  - Recipe Hacks for a Box of Mac & Cheese